HBJ TREASURY OF LITERATURE

DANCE TO THE MUSIC

SENIOR AUTHORS
ROGER C. FARR
DOROTHY S. STRICKLAND

AUTHORS
RICHARD F. ABRAHAMSON
ELLEN BOOTH CHURCH
BARBARA BOWEN COULTER
MARGARET A. GALLEGO
JUDITH L. IRVIN
KAREN KUTIPER
JUNKO YOKOTA LEWIS
DONNA M. OGLE
TIMOTHY SHANAHAN
PATRICIA SMITH

SENIOR CONSULTANTS
BERNICE E. CULLINAN
W. DORSEY HAMMOND
ASA G. HILLIARD III

CONSULTANTS
ALONZO A. CRIM
ROLANDO R. HINOJOSA-SMITH
LEE BENNETT HOPKINS
ROBERT J. STERNBERG

 HARCOURT BRACE JOVANOVICH, INC.
Orlando Austin San Diego Chicago Dallas New York

Requests for permission to make copies of any part of the work should be mailed to: Permissions Department, Harcourt Brace Jovanovich, Publishers, 8th Floor, Orlando, Florida 32887

Printed in the United States of America

ISBN 0-15-300421-5

2 3 4 5 6 7 8 9 10   048   96 95 94 93

Acknowledgments

For permission to reprint copyrighted material, grateful acknowledgment is made to the following sources:

Dutton Children's Books, a division of Penguin Books USA Inc.: Tonight Is Carnaval by Arthur Dorros, illustrated with arpilleras sewn by the Club de Madres Virgen del Carmen of Lima, Peru. Text copyright © 1991 by Arthur Dorros; illustrations copyright © 1991 by Dutton Children's Books. *Matthew and Tilly* by Rebecca C. Jones, illustrated by Beth Peck. Text copyright © 1991 by Rebecca C. Jones; illustrations copyright © 1991 by Beth Peck.

HarperCollins Publishers: Poinsettia & Her Family by Felicia Bond. Copyright © 1981 by Felicia Bond. Published by Thomas Y. Crowell.

Henry Holt and Company, Inc.: Mr. McGill Goes to Town by Jim Aylesworth, illustrated by Thomas Graham. Text copyright © 1989 by Jim Aylesworth; illustrations copyright © 1989 by Thomas Graham.

Lothrop, Lee & Shepard Books, a division of William Morrow & Company, Inc.: The Best Friends Club: A Lizzie and Harold Story by Elizabeth Winthrop, illustrated by Martha Weston. Text copyright © 1989 by Elizabeth Winthrop; illustrations copyright © 1989 by Martha Weston.

Parents Magazine Press, a division of Gruner & Jahr USA Publishing: Henry Goes West by Robert Quackenbush. Copyright © 1982 by Robert Quackenbush.

Photo Credits

Key: (t) top, (b) bottom, (l) left, (c) center, (r) right.

6, HBJ Photo; 30, HBJ Photo; 57, Dennis Fagan; 58, HBJ Photo; 86, HBJ Photo; 132, HBJ Photo; 158(l), Courtesy, HarperCollins Publishing; 158(t), David Brownell/The Image Bank; 158(b), Francisco Hidalgo/The Image Bank; 166, Andre Gallant/The Image Bank.

Illustration Credits

Key: (t) top, (b) bottom, (l) left, (c) center, (r) right.

Table of Contents Art

Roseanne Litzinger, 4 (bl); Gerald McDermott, 5 (br); Sue Williams, 4 (tl), 4–5 (c).

Unit Opening Patterns

Dan Thoner

Selection Art

Thomas Graham, 7–29; Felicia Bond, 31–55; Martha Weston, 59–85; Beth Peck, 87–107; Robert Quackenbush, 108–131; Club de Madres Virgen del Carmen, 133–155.

Dear Reader,

In this book, there is a boy who loves to play music. He can't wait to be part of the celebration. He can't wait to see everyone dance to the music. Turn on your imagination. You are invited to join the happy celebration!

As you read these stories, you'll meet a lot of different people, all with very different problems to solve. Read about people from long ago who work together and help each other. Read another story about Poinsettia. This time she has a problem with her family. Meet friends who have fights but still like each other very much. Have a wild adventure out West! Then go all the way to South America to meet a boy and his family. Let your imagination dance as you celebrate "Carnaval" with them!

Get to know the people and their cultures. Get to know the characters. You may find out you have a lot in common. Then get ready for more stories, more friends, and more adventures. Come right in! Feel the beat and let the fun begin!

Sincerely,
The Authors

DANCE TO THE MUSIC

DANCE·TO·THE·MUSIC

C O N T E N T S

UNIT THREE/NEIGHBORHOODS

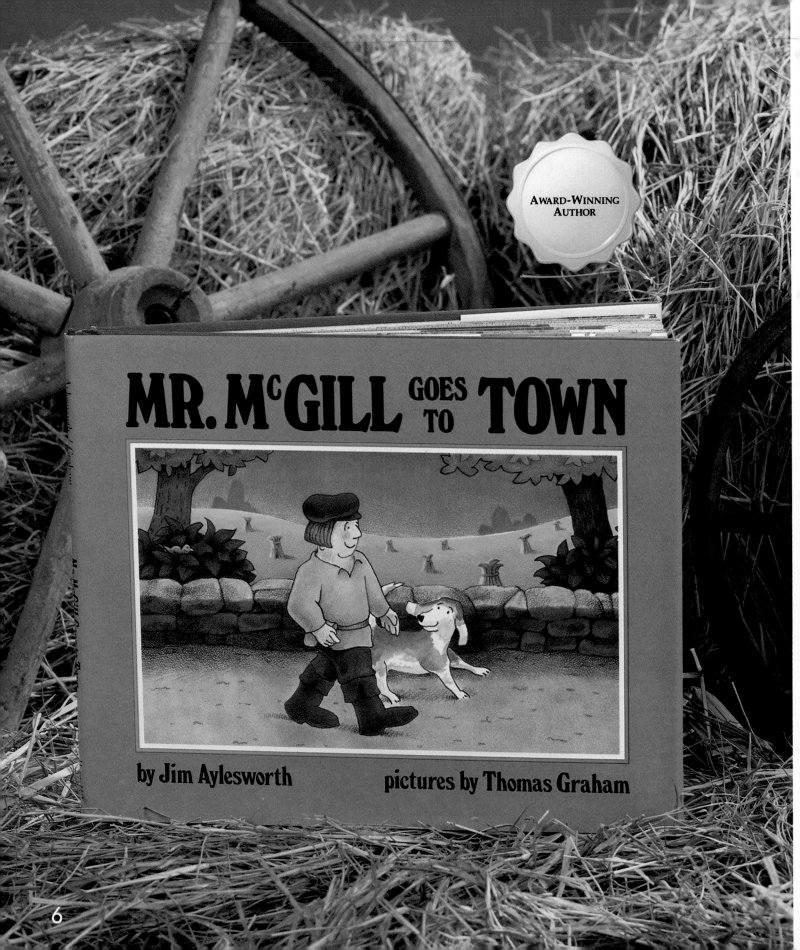

MR. McGILL GOES TO TOWN

by Jim Aylesworth

pictures by Thomas Graham

Early one morning Mr. McGill began work on repairs to his mill. It was very hot.

He worked very hard, but before long he sat down by the stream with a sigh.

"Ohhh. . . . With so much to do, I may never get through. I've got to get help, or the sun will go down and I won't get to town."

So he walked through the field, to where Mr. McRae
was cutting his hay.

"If you will," said Mr. McGill, "I could sure use some help repairing my mill."

"I'll do as you say," said Mr. McRae, "if you'll just help me cut my hay."

"I will," said McGill, and the two friends went right to work.

They worked very hard, but before long they leaned on their tools, and they sighed.

"Ohhh. . . . This job is real rough. There's too much of this stuff. We've got to get help, or the sun will go down and we won't get to town."

So they walked across the road, to where Mr. McCall was building a wall.

12

"If you will," said Mr. McGill, "I could sure use some help repairing my mill."

"And cutting my hay," added Mr. McRae.

"No trouble at all," said Mr. McCall, "if you'll just help me build my wall."

"We will," said McGill, and the three friends went right to work.

They worked very hard, but before long they sat on
a stone, and they sighed.

"Ohhh. . . . We know we are strong, but this wall is
too long. We've got to get help, or the sun will go down
and we won't get to town."

So they walked over the bridge, to where Mr. McNeil
was fixing a wheel.

"If you will," said Mr. McGill, "I could sure use some help repairing my mill."

"And cutting my hay," said Mr. McRae.

"And building my wall," added Mr. McCall.

"I'll make a deal," said Mr. McNeil, "if you'll just help me fix my wheel."

"We will," said McGill, and the four friends went right to work.

They worked very hard, but before long they lay in
the grass, and they sighed.

"Ohhh. . . . This wheel's really broke. It isn't a joke.
We've got to get help, or the sun will go down and we
won't get to town."

So they walked down the lane, to where Mr. McGrew
was nailing a shoe.

"If you will," said Mr. McGill, "I could sure use some help repairing my mill."

"And cutting my hay," said Mr. McRae.

"And building my wall," said Mr. McCall.

"And fixing my wheel," added Mr. McNeil.

"That's what I'll do," said Mr. McGrew, "if you'll just help me nail this shoe."

"We will!" said McGill, and the five friends went right to work.

And with so many to help, it was easy to nail that shoe, and the other three too.

Then they led the horse back up the lane and fixed
the wheel.

Then they hitched the horse to the wagon

and rode back over the bridge to build the wall.

Then they drove across the road to cut the hay

and rattled through the field to repair the mill.

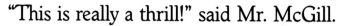

They worked so well that the sun was still high in the sky. So they washed in the stream and went to town.

"This is really a thrill!" said Mr. McGill.

"A wonderful day!" said Mr. McRae.

"I'm loving it all!" said Mr. McCall.

"I know how you feel!" said Mr. McNeil.

"That goes for me, too!" said Mr. McGrew.

Then when they were done, they sat out of the sun,
where Mr. McQuade served them cool lemonade.
Ahhh. . . .

POINSETTIA
&
HER FAMILY

AWARD-WINNING
AUTHOR

Felicia Bond

Poinsettia had six brothers and sisters, a mother, and a father.

They lived in a fine, old house surrounded by hydrangea bushes and lilac hedges, which Poinsettia's mother would occasionally cut for a nice effect in the dining room.

There was pachysandra in which to play
hide-and-seek in the early evenings of summer, and
a rock out front to sit on.

Inside, there was a red leather window seat for
reading in the late afternoon sun, and a bathroom
with balloon-pink wallpaper. Poinsettia thought it a
perfect house.

One day, Poinsettia came home from the library with her favorite book, a book about a little, spotted circus horse who danced. Poinsettia had read it five times before, but she was looking forward to it all the same.

She trotted past her mother in the garden and her father in the kitchen, and headed straight for the red leather window seat.

If the sun was coming in the window just right, it would spread like warm butter across the pages of her book. Poinsettia walked a little faster, patting her pocket to make sure it held the cherry tart she had bought for just this occasion.

The sun was coming in the window just right,
but it was spreading like warm butter across the fat,
little body of Julius, the third from the youngest,
who was already curled up on the soft red leather.

"I will go to the rock in the front yard," Poinsettia grunted, "where I can read my book in peace."

But the rock could hardly be seen for all the piglets lying about. "Like a bunch of seals," Poinsettia snorted.

She stomped off toward the balloon-pink
bathroom, where the tub was just right for reading.
But there, up to her chins in water, was Chick Pea,
who said she hadn't washed her feet yet.

"This house would be perfect except for one
thing," Poinsettia fumed. "There are too many of
us in it! It is not possible to go anywhere without
running into a brother or a sister, a mother or a
father!"

That night, Poinsettia was very nasty. She pinched a brother, stepped on a sister, and yelled louder than both of them put together.

She did more things and worse things, and it was only seven o'clock.

Poinsettia was sent to bed early that night for general misbehavior.

The next day, Poinsettia's father announced to the whole family that they were moving. "We will look for a new house," he said. "This one is too small for us."

"Oh, no, it's not," Poinsettia thought. "It's the family that's too big." But she kept her thoughts to herself and vowed not to go with them.

When the family left, Poinsettia lay low in the pachysandra. Nobody noticed. The car seemed full.

She lay there a long time, just in case they came back. They didn't.

"Good!" Poinsettia said and, clutching her book close to her, ran straight for the red leather window seat.

The light had never been more buttery, nor the leather as warm. Poinsettia read two pages there, then ran to the rock in the front yard. The rock had never felt more solid.

Poinsettia read six more pages. But a wind was whipping up, and it was even starting to snow.
Poinsettia ran inside.

She warmed herself in a deliciously hot bath.
She read four pages, then spent an hour staring
dreamily at the wallpaper. It had never looked
pinker, and neither had Poinsettia.

"I'm a pig in bliss," she gurgled.

Poinsettia let the water out of the tub.

The snow came down harder, and Poinsettia fell asleep. She dreamed about the dancing circus horse.

It snowed all that afternoon and into the evening. By the time it was dark, Poinsettia had read her book eighteen times. She wrapped herself in an old blanket and looked for something to eat. What little food there was she ate cold.

"The house is not as it used to be," she said aloud quietly.

"What I need is a rope! If I had a rope, I could make a tent with this blanket. I could tie the rope to two doorknobs and put the blanket over it. My tent would be a house inside a house. What a good idea."

Poinsettia searched everywhere for a bit of rope. All she found was a frayed piece of string that was barely long enough for anything.

But in the farthest corner of a dark, dark closet, Poinsettia found something else. It was a photograph, an old photograph of her family. Poinsettia remembered taking it herself.

This was too much for Poinsettia.

With the point of her hoof, she very carefully made a little hole in the top of the photograph. Through the hole she threaded the string she had found. On each end she made a knot.

"This is all I have left of my family!" Poinsettia
cried, and cried, and cried.

"Poinsettia!" a small voice called. "Poinsettia!"
Poinsettia nearly fainted dead away.

There were her six brothers and sisters, her mother and her father, all squashed and crowded together and smiling from ear to ear!

"We would have been back sooner," Poinsettia's father said, "but the car got stuck in the snow. It's a good thing there are so many of us. We all got out and pushed."

"Pierre counted everyone, but he counted wrong because he's only three," said Petunia, the oldest.

"I don't know why we didn't notice right away that you were missing," Julius said, "because everything was so peaceful."

"The whole time we were gone, Poinsettia," her mother said, "we talked about what a wonderful house this is. It is our home. Perhaps we don't need as much room as we thought."

"Maybe not," Poinsettia said.

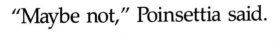

And shoulder to shoulder, elbow to elbow, all
squashed and crowded together, they spent the rest
of that night, and many other nights together . . .
as together as nine pigs could be . . .

in their fine, old house.

Felicia P Bond

Poinsettia's family is based on my own family. I am the second oldest of seven children. We lived in a big old house just outside of New York City. I loved that house. It had a little rock in the front yard. That house did not have a red window seat, but when I was five or six, we did live in a house with that window seat. I remember seeing light pour in over the window seat. It was so beautiful! At that moment I knew I wanted to be an artist.

My family laughs when they read about Poinsettia because they don't think I've changed much.

"This house would be perfect except for one thing," Poinsettia fumed. "There are too many of us in it! It is not possible to go anywhere without running into a brother or a sister, a mother or a father!"

I remember wishing I were in a smaller family because it was so noisy. That's the worst thing about a large family— the noise. I like lots of people around and I'm close to my family. But the noise bothered me, so I was kind of mean and bossy. The best thing about a big family is that there's always someone to play with.

Do you remember that in the story, Poinsettia wears a photograph around her neck? I got the idea from something that happened when I lived in New York City. It was Christmas and I wasn't going home. I took out all my photographs and put them on my tree. That was how I celebrated with my family, even though I couldn't be with them. The story I wrote wasn't about Christmas. But my main character's name, Poinsettia, put a little bit of Christmas into the story anyway.

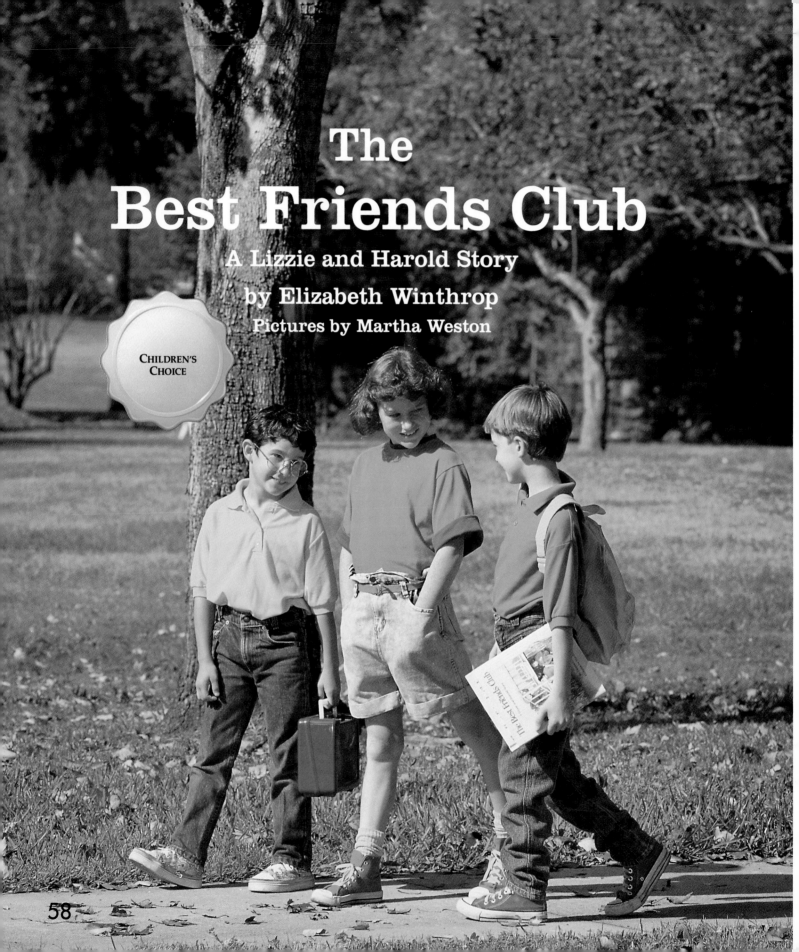

The
Best Friends Club

A Lizzie and Harold Story

by Elizabeth Winthrop
Pictures by Martha Weston

CHILDREN'S
CHOICE

Lizzie and Harold were best friends.

Harold taught Lizzie how to do cat's cradle.

Lizzie taught Harold how to play running bases.

Lizzie shared her trick-or-treat candy with Harold,
and Harold let Lizzie ride his big red bike.

They always walked home from school together.

"Let's start a best friends club," Lizzie said one day.

"Great," said Harold. "We can meet under your porch.
That will be our clubhouse."

Harold painted the sign.
It said
THE BF CLUB.

"Now write *Members Only*," said Lizzie.

"You write it," said Harold. "My teacher says my M's are too fat."

So Lizzie wrote *Members Only*.

"Who are the members?" Harold asked.

"You and me," said Lizzie.

"That's all?"

"Yes," said Lizzie. "You can be the president and I'll be the vice-president. The president gets to write down all the rules."

"You be the president," Harold said. "Your writing is better than mine."

"All right, then I'll be president," said Lizzie. "Now we'll make up the rules."

"Rule number one," said Harold. "The club meets under Lizzie's porch."

"Right," said Lizzie. "Rule number two. Nobody else can be in the club."

"Rule number three," said Harold. He thought for a long time. "I can't think of any more."

"Rule number three," said Lizzie. "Lizzie and Harold walk home from school together every day."

"Rule number four," said Harold. "Everybody in the club knows cat's cradle."

They heard voices. Someone was walking by. They could see two pairs of feet.

"It's Christina," whispered Lizzie. "She always wears those black party shoes."

"And Douglas," Harold whispered back. "His shoelaces are always untied."

"I'm only having Nancy and Amy and Stacey to my birthday party," they heard Christina say.

"My mother said I could have my whole class," Douglas answered. "We're going to play baseball."

"Oh goody," said Harold. "That means I'll be invited to Douglas's birthday party."

"I won't," Lizzie said gloomily. She was in a different class.

The next day, Harold came out of his classroom with
Douglas.

"He wants to walk home with us," Harold said to
Lizzie.

"He can't," said Lizzie.

"Why not?" asked Harold.

"Harold, remember the rules. We're best friends and we
always walk home together," Lizzie said. "Just you and me."

"Oh yeah," said Harold. "I forgot."
Douglas looked very sad.
"Sorry, Douglas," Harold said. "See you tomorrow."

"Douglas's ears stick out," Lizzie said on the way home.

"So what?" said Harold.

"His shoelaces are always dripping," said Lizzie.

"I don't care about that," said Harold.

"I'll meet you in the clubhouse after snacks," said Lizzie.

"I can't come today," said Harold. "My mother wants me home."

Lizzie sat in the clubhouse all by herself.

She wrote down more rules.

They said

5. Best friends don't go to other people's birthday parties.

6. People with funny ears and drippy shoelaces are not allowed in the club.

The next day, Harold came out of his classroom with Douglas again.

"Douglas asked me to play at his house," said Harold.

"*Harold,*" said Lizzie. "What about the club?"

"What club?" asked Douglas.

"None of your business," said Lizzie.

"I'll come tomorrow," said Harold. "I promise."

Lizzie watched them walk away together. She stuck out her tongue at them, but Harold didn't turn around.

She went straight to the clubhouse and wrote down another rule. It said

7. Best friends don't go to other people's houses to play.

Then she threw a ball at the garage wall until suppertime.

"Douglas wants to be in the club," said Harold the next day.

"He can't be," said Lizzie. "Only best friends are allowed in this club."

She showed him all the new rules she had written down.

"This club is no fun," said Harold. "It has too many rules. I quit."

He crawled out from under the porch and walked home.
Lizzie took down his sign and put up a new one.

Douglas came down the street.

He was riding Harold's new bicycle.

Harold was chasing after him.

When Harold saw the sign, he stopped and read it.

"What does it say?" asked Douglas.

"It says, 'Lizzie's Club. Nobody Else Allowed,'" Harold said.

Harold leaned over and looked at Lizzie. "You can't have a club with only one person," he said.

"*I* can," said Lizzie.

"A three-person club is more fun," said Harold. "Douglas knows how to do cat's cradle."

"But he's not a best friend," said Lizzie.

"It'll be a different kind of club," said Harold. "We'll make up a new name."

"Maybe," said Lizzie.

78

She sat under the porch and watched them.
First they played bicycle tag.
Then they threw the ball at her garage wall.

"Want to play running bases?" Lizzie asked.

"I don't know how," said Douglas.

"I'll teach you," said Lizzie.

They took turns being the runner. Lizzie was the fastest.

Douglas whispered something to Harold.

"Douglas wants you to come to his birthday party," said Harold.

Then Lizzie whispered something to Harold.

"Lizzie says yes," Harold said to Douglas.

"And I've thought of a new name for the club," said Lizzie. "Douglas can be in it too."

"Oh boy!" said Douglas.

"You can be the first member. I am the president and Harold is the vice-president," said Lizzie.

"That's okay with me," said Harold.

"Me too," said Douglas.

It was getting dark.

Douglas went home for supper.

Lizzie crawled back under the porch. She tore up her sign and her list of rules.

"What's the new name for the club?" Harold asked.

"I'll show you," said Lizzie.

She sat down and wrote in great big letters
THE NO RULES CLUB.

Harold smiled.
He stuck up the sign with a thumbtack.
Then they both went upstairs to Lizzie's house for supper.

MATTHEW AND TILLY

by Rebecca C. Jones

Illustrated by Beth Peck

NOTABLE CHILDREN'S
TRADE BOOK IN THE
FIELD OF SOCIAL
STUDIES

MATTHEW and TILLY were friends.

They rode bikes together,

and they played hide-and-seek together.

They sold lemonade together.

When business was slow, they played sidewalk games together.

And sometimes they ate ice-cream cones together.

Once they even rescued a lady's

kitten from a tree together.

The lady gave them money for the bubble-gum machines.
So later they chewed gum together and remembered how
brave they had been.

Sometimes, though, Matthew and Tilly got sick of each other.

One day when they were coloring, Matthew broke Tilly's purple crayon. He didn't mean to, but he did.

"You broke my crayon," Tilly said in her crabbiest voice.

"It was an old crayon," Matthew said in his grouchiest voice. "It was ready to break."

"No, it wasn't," Tilly said. "It was a brand-new crayon, and you broke it. You always break everything."

"Stop being so picky," Matthew said. "You're always so picky and stinky and mean."

"Well, you're so stupid," Tilly said. "You're so stupid and stinky and mean."

Matthew stomped up the stairs. By himself.

Tilly found a piece of chalk and began drawing numbers and squares on the sidewalk. By herself.

Upstairs, Matthew got out his cash register and some cans so he could play store. He piled the cans extra high, and he put prices on everything. This was the best store he had ever made. Probably because that picky and stinky and mean old Tilly wasn't around to mess it up.

But he didn't have a customer. And playing store wasn't much fun without a customer.

Tilly finished drawing the numbers and squares. She drew them really big, with lots of squiggly lines. This was the best sidewalk game she had ever drawn. Probably because that stupid and stinky and mean old Matthew wasn't around to mess it up.

But she didn't have anyone to play with. And a sidewalk game wasn't much fun without another player.

Matthew looked out the window and wondered what Tilly was doing. Tilly looked up at Matthew's window and wondered what he was doing.

She smiled, just a little. That was enough for Matthew.

"I'm sorry," he called.

"So am I," said Tilly.

And Matthew ran downstairs so they could play.

Together again.

HENRY GOES WEST

by Robert Quackenbush

AWARD-WINNING
AUTHOR

Henry the Duck missed his friend Clara, who was vacationing out West. He decided to pay her a surprise visit. So he packed his bag and took the first plane heading West to meet her.

Henry arrived at Clara's guest ranch early the
next morning. But the ranch was closed.
Everyone had just left for an all-day trail ride.
They would not be back until midnight.

Henry decided to have a look around the ranch while he waited for Clara. As he was snapping a picture near the barn, Henry backed right into a mule.

The surprised mule kicked Henry!
Henry landed on the back of a horse.

The horse was a
bucking bronco!
Henry was taken
for a wild ride.
Then he was tossed
over a fence.

Henry landed in a bull's pen!
The bull chased Henry.
Henry ran and ran.

At last Henry got out of the bull's pen.
He went to sit on a large rock. But he did
not see the cactus behind it. Henry sat down
on the cactus!

Henry jumped up and quacked loudly.
The noise frightened some cattle
grazing nearby.

The cattle began running. Soon they were racing at full speed. Henry had started a stampede!

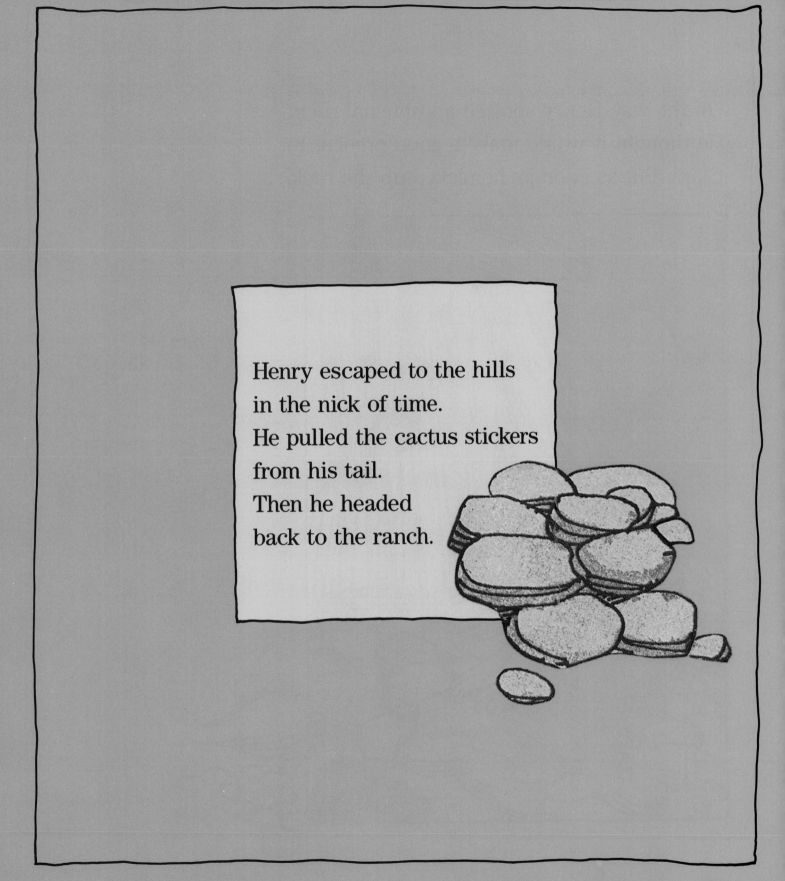

Henry escaped to the hills
in the nick of time.
He pulled the cactus stickers
from his tail.
Then he headed
back to the ranch.

On the way, Henry spotted an unusual rock.
He thought it would make a good present for
Clara. But as soon as he picked up the rock . . .

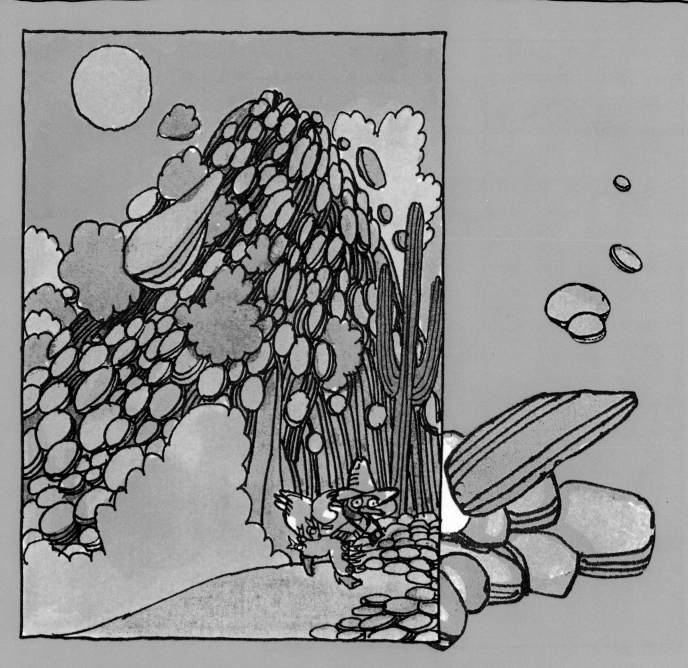

he heard a loud rumbling from the mountaintop.
Henry had started a landslide!
He ran as fast as he could go.

Henry got clear of the landslide. Then he went
straight back to the ranch to wait for Clara.

Henry waited and waited. It was turning cold
on the desert. So Henry built a campfire.
He stood close to the fire to warm his
tail feathers. Too close.

Suddenly, Henry's
tail feathers
began to sizzle!
He made a beeline
for the water
and dove in.

Henry was soaking wet and all worn out.
He wished Clara would hurry up and get there.

At last the riding party returned. But Clara was not with them. Henry asked one of the cowboys if he had seen her.

"Sorry, mister," said the cowboy . . .

"Clara went home yesterday. She said she was lonesome for someone named Henry."

NOTABLE CHILDREN'S TRADE BOOK IN THE FIELD OF SOCIAL STUDIES

TONIGHT IS CARNAVAL

BY ARTHUR DORROS

Illustrated with *arpilleras* sewn by the Club de Madres ... a, Peru

Wake up, sleepyhead," my mother is calling. But I'm already awake. I'm thinking about Carnaval. This year I will play the *quena,* a flute, with my father in the band. "The quena is the voice of the band—the singer of the band," says Papa. Papa plays with the band every year at Carnaval. People in costumes will parade and dance to the music for three whole days and nights.

Carnaval is in the big village down the valley, and it's only three days away!

"We have a lot of work to do before then," Papa says. We work all year, almost every day, but not during Carnaval!

We get up each day before it is light outside, there is so much to do. Mama takes my little sister, Teresa, to the river to get water. Today Mama washes clothes, too. Papa and I look for firewood to use for cooking. Sometimes we walk a long way to find wood—there are hardly any trees in the high Andes Mountains of South America, where we live.

Today I bring my quena along, so I can practice special songs for Carnaval. A lot of the songs have a good beat that makes you want to dance. *Tunk tunk, tunk tunk.* Papa's ax chopping a log sounds like the beat of the *bombo,* the drum he will play with the band.

Back home Teresa drops kernels of corn into an empty pot. Mama will boil the corn for our meal. *Pling pling, pling pling pling.* The kernels make sounds like the strings of Uncle Pablo's *charango.* He will play in the band with us too, at Carnaval.

After our meal, we get a field ready for planting. I lead the oxen, to make sure they plow straight. Mama follows us and picks stones out of the loose earth. After Carnaval, my friend Paco and his family will help us plant potatoes. Sometimes Paco's family helps us in our field, and other times we help them in theirs. One of the songs I'm practicing for Carnaval is about working in the fields with friends.

137

After we plow, I take the hungry llamas high into the mountains to find grass. The best grass is by the crumbling walls of buildings made hundreds of years ago when the Incas ruled these mountains. No one knows how the giant stones were cut to fit together so well. Sometimes we use the old stones to build walls and houses and even terraces for the fields.

I sit on a wall and play my quena. I play a song called *"Mis Llamitas,"* "My Little Llamas," and the llamas leap and dance around. I imagine they are dancing to my music.

The wind whistling across the stones sounds like the windy notes of a *zampoña,* a panpipe. I will play my quena and Paco will play his zampoña when we meet at Carnaval. That's one of the things I like about Carnaval—we get together with friends from our mountain and from all around the valley.

One day is gone. Now we have only today and tomorrow before tomorrow night—when Carnaval begins. I can hardly wait. This morning Papa shears wool from an alpaca. An alpaca is like a llama, but with softer wool. I carry the wool to Mama, so she can spin it into yarn. "You don't have to run," laughs Mama. "Carnaval will come as soon as it can."

Mama's fingers twirl the wool round and round. She can spin yarn while she's walking, or selling vegetables, or doing almost anything. When she has enough yarn, she'll color it with different dyes. Grandma will weave it into cloth of many colors. Then Mama will cut and sew the cloth to make us clothes. Maybe she'll make me a new jacket.

143

144

In the afternoon, we dig potatoes out of the damp earth in a field we planted months ago. The digging usually makes me tired, but today I keep working as fast as I can to help harvest all the potatoes. Tomorrow we'll take them down into the valley to sell at the market. And after the market is cleared away, Carnaval will begin!

We gather red potatoes; yellow, black, and brown potatoes; even purple potatoes. In the Andes, we have hundreds of different kinds of potatoes.

We drop our potatoes into burlap bags, *plonk, plonk, plonk*. The llamas help carry the heavy bags to Antonio's truck. Antonio came from the village today, and he will sleep tonight in his truck.

Finally. Today we take the potatoes to market—then tonight is Carnaval!

I wait and wait to hear the truck start. The motor coughs and groans, *errr errr errr.* But at last Antonio gets it started. Mama, Papa, Teresa, and I—and the potatoes— bounce along in the back of the old truck, which rattles and shakes down the mountain. It stops like a bus to pick up people carrying onions, beans, carrots, turnips, peas, and peppers; llama wool; clothes; and food they have made for Carnaval.

"Hey," I hear someone say, "don't let that chicken eat our corn. We're taking it to market."

The truck bounces over a big bump. I reach down to make sure my quena is not broken. I want people to hear my quena sing when I play at Carnaval.

"Watch out flying over those bumps, Antonio," someone shouts. "Will this old truck fly us to the village?"

"Don't worry," Antonio shouts back. "This old truck and I know how to get there."

People hug when they climb into the truck. We don't see these friends very often. We all stand and look out along the way. People throw water balloons and water from buckets to try to splash us. They're excited about Carnaval.

At the market, I help unload the heavy bags of potatoes, and then I walk around. I love to see the brightly colored piles of vegetables. People trade wool that still smells like llamas or sheep. And the nutty smell of toasted fava beans and corn makes my mouth water.

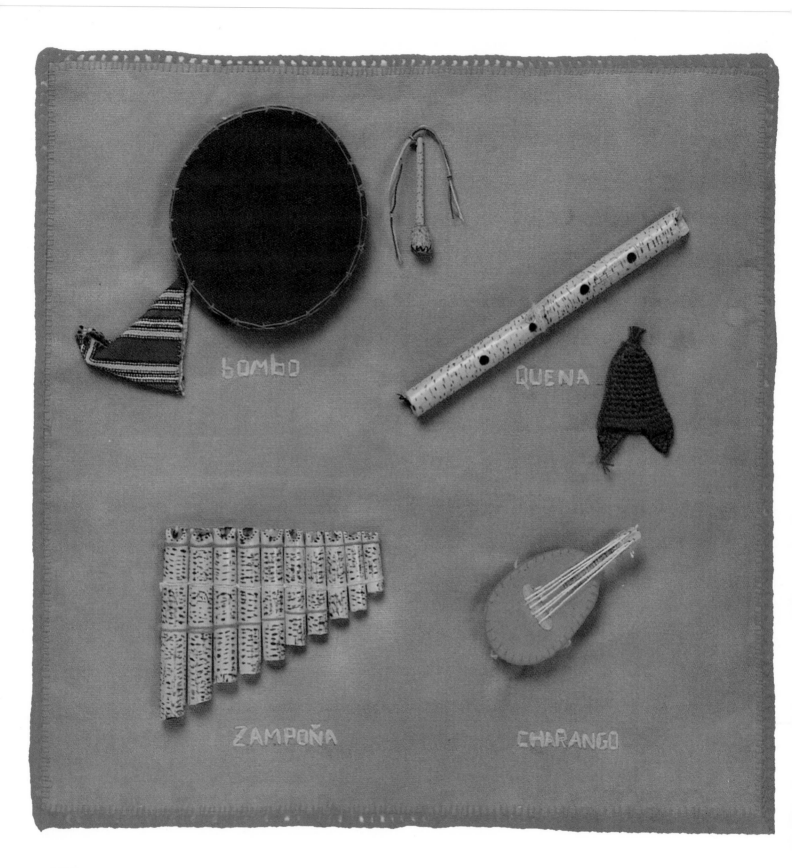

bombo

QUENA

ZAMPOÑA

CHARANGO

But today I can't wait until Mama sells all of our potatoes and the market is cleared away. Then people will come out in their costumes. At first it will be hard to see who each person is—many of the people will be wearing masks. I'll find the band. Papa's bombo will start booming, Paco's zampoña will be whistling, and Uncle Pablo's charango plinging. People will start shouting "Play your songs," stamping their feet, swirling, turning, dancing to the music faster and faster because—

TONIGHT IS CARNAVAL.

154

When I play my quena with the band, people start to sing. My quena sings and the people sing. I play the special songs I've learned for Carnaval, about llamas, mountains, and friends. We play songs with a beat for dancing. Paco and I watch all the people hold onto each other in one long line that dances—laughing, winding through the village.

Our band plays under the moon and flickering stars, and we will play until the sun comes up. We play the songs of our mountain days and nights . . . for tonight is Carnaval.

HOW ARPILLERAS ARE MADE

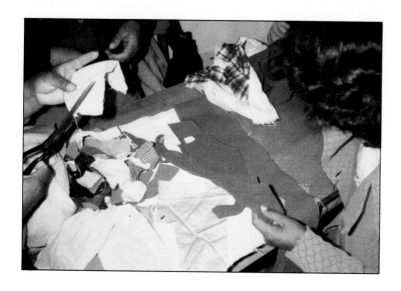

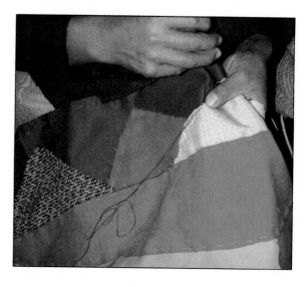

An arpillera-maker draws the design on white cloth. Pieces of cloth are selected and cut to fit the design.

Big pieces of cloth are sewn on to form the background.

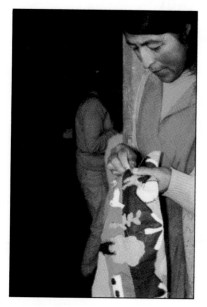

The edges of each shape are neatly stitched, and details are added by sewing on more pieces of cut cloth and by embroidering.

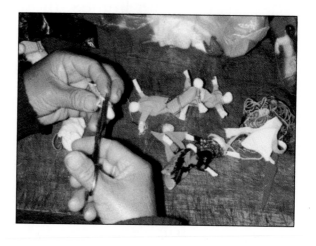

Dolls and other three-dimensional objects (vegetables, musical instruments) are made...

. . . and sewn onto the arpillera.

Another arpillera is finished.

Arpillera-makers often work together in groups. These members of the Club de Madres Virgen del Carmen are making vegetables and dolls for arpilleras. With money from the sale of arpilleras, the group also runs a kitchen that helps feed two to three hundred people a day.

Words from the Author: ARTHUR DORROS

In 1975, I was traveling in South America. One day, in Peru, the bus I was riding on broke down, so everyone had to get out while the driver fixed it. We were up 15,000 feet in the mountains. The air is very thin at that height, and I got a little dizzy. I went to sit down around a bend in the road, and below me I heard a shepherd. He was playing a flute to his llamas. That picture stuck in my mind and was the seed for my book Tonight Is Carnaval. By the way, I almost missed the bus because I was so busy listening to the music!

Another experience helped me get more ideas for my story. I was riding in an open-back truck across the high plains of the Andes Mountains. It was carnival time. As we got near a town, we would see bands warming up in the fields. Then we would go into a town, and a carnival would be going on. Now, I wanted to put a carnival in my story.

Even though I am an artist as well as a writer, I did not want to draw the pictures for this book. I was happy when the book's editor told me about folk art from South America called **arpilleras.** Arpillera means "burlap" in Spanish. Long ago, the colorful pictures were sewn onto sackcloth. I thought that arpilleras would make good pictures for the book. But, it was hard to find the people who make them. Most of these people are poor and don't have telephones. Happily, I did find a group to work with.

First, I wrote the story from what I knew about life in the Andes Mountains. Then, the arpillera group made the pictures for the book. We worked together very well.

The cloth arpilleras have been sold, and the money was given to the villagers to help them live better lives.

GLOSSARY

The **Glossary** can help you understand what words mean. It gives the meaning of a word as it is used in the story. It also has an example sentence to show how to use the word in a sentence.

The words in the **Glossary** are in ABC order. ABC order is also called **alphabetical order.** To find a word, you must remember the order of the letters of the alphabet.

Suppose you wanted to find *crowded* in the **Glossary.** First, you find the **C** words. **C** comes near the beginning of the alphabet, so the **C** words must be near the beginning of the **Glossary.** Then, use the guide words at the top of the page to help you find the entry word *crowded.* It is on page 162.

A **synonym,** or word that has the same meaning, sometimes comes after an example sentence. It is shown as *syn.*

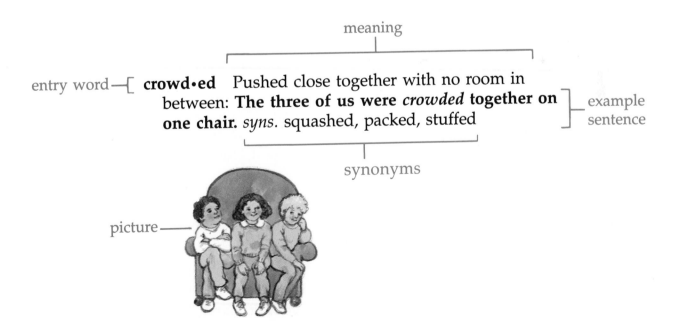

meaning

entry word —[**crowd•ed**   Pushed close together with no room in between: **The three of us were** *crowded* **together on one chair.** *syns.* squashed, packed, stuffed

example sentence

synonyms

picture —

A

ar·rived Came to a place after a trip: **They *arrived* at Grandmother's house after driving for five hours.** *syn.* reached

crowded

B

bee·line The shortest way from one place to another: **When it started to rain, Takeo made a *beeline* for the door so he wouldn't get wet.**

brave Willing to do something even if you are afraid: **Ben thought Tamara was *brave* because she didn't even blink when she got a shot at the doctor's office.** *syn.* bold

busi·ness Work that is done to make money: **Maria earned money from her pet-sitting *business*.**

dyes

C

crowd·ed Pushed close together with no room in between: **The three of us were *crowded* together on one chair.** *syns.* squashed, packed, stuffed

D

dyes Materials used to color yarn or cloth: **We use *dyes* to turn the white wool red and blue.**

es·caped   Went somewhere to be safe or get free: **The rabbit *escaped* to the bushes, where it was safe.**

guest   A person who has come to visit: **When Grandpa visits, he sleeps in our *guest* room.**

harvest

har·vest   To pick or gather ripe crops: **We *harvest* the oranges so that people can eat them.**

im·ag·ine   To make believe: **Annie likes to *imagine* that the birds know what she is saying to them as she sits in her tree house.** *syn.* pretend

leaned

leaned   Rested against something: **The man *leaned* against the pole to rest.**

lone·some   Feeling sad because someone is not there: **Juanita is always *lonesome* for her father when he is away.**

M

market

mar·ket A place where many kinds of things are bought and sold: **At the** *market* **in our town square, Steven bought cheese, tomatoes, and candles.**

mem·bers People who belong to a group: **Rosa and Susan became** *members* **of the school band because they love to play music.**

P

peace·ful Calm and quiet; no fighting: **When my cousins stopped yelling and fighting, the house was** *peaceful.*

prom·ise To say to someone that you will do something and mean it: **If I** *promise* **to play at Erika's house today, that is where I will go.**

R

repairs

re·pairs What you do to fix something: **After Dan made** *repairs* **to the broken toaster, it worked again.**

res·cued Saved from something bad: **In the fairy tale, the prince** *rescued* **the princess from the castle where she was locked up.** *syn.* freed

rough Hard to do: **Making a path through the deep snow was** *rough* **work for my little brother.**

S

shears   Cuts hair or wool from: **The barber says Mark's hair is as thick as the wool that his brother *shears* from sheep.** *syn.* shaves

sigh   A deep, loud breath you let out when you are tired or sad: **I heard Ramon give a *sigh* because he could not find his lost puppy.**

spread   To move or stretch out across: **The spilled milk *spread* across the kitchen floor in a big puddle.**

stomped   Took big, heavy steps that make noise: **Kiko was so angry that she *stomped* across the porch and made it shake.** *syn.* stamped

straight   Without stopping or wandering around: **My mom told me to come *straight* home from school without stopping to visit my friend.**

sur·round·ed   Circled around by something: **Since the camp is *surrounded* by trees, we see trees wherever we look.**

T

tore   Ripped: **Chen *tore* the newspaper into tiny pieces to put in his hamster's cage.**

spread

surrounded

tore

un·u·su·al   Not usual, not like others: **Most cats have long tails, but this *unusual* cat has a very short tail.**

valley

val·ley   Low land between hills or mountains: **In summer the air is cooler on the hilltops than it is down in the *valley*.**

vil·lage   A small town in the country: **The people who live in Pedro's *village* have small houses with enough land around them for growing vegetables.**

whis·pered   Spoke in a low, quiet voice: **Mrs. Carson *whispered* to Jon so that no one else could hear what she said.**

won·dered   Wanted to know: **George left without telling us, so we *wondered* where he had gone.**

whispered